Separate Ways

Story by Dawn McMillan
Illustrations by Meredith Thomas

Tess and Nathan were worried. There was something happening in their family that they didn't understand. Mom and Dad were often very quiet, and sometimes Mom's eyes were red from crying.

One morning, Tess asked, "What's wrong, Mom?"

Nathan whispered anxiously, "Are you sick?"

"I'm all right ... just a bit tired, that's all," Mom replied, with a tremble in her voice.

Dad was tired, too. He didn't laugh and joke the way he used to. After he got home from work, he was too exhausted to play football or basketball.

"Come on, Dad!" begged Nathan. "Come outside with us!"

"Just for a while, please," said Tess.

"Perhaps tomorrow," sighed Dad, and after dinner he sat down in front of the television and went to sleep.

Tess and Nathan went to their bedrooms and tried to read. Later, they heard Mom and Dad talking in hushed voices.

Nathan knocked on Tess's door and called softly, "Tess, there is something wrong!"

He went in and sat on the end of the bed. "Mom and Dad don't seem to like each other any more!" he said.

"I wonder what's going to happen," sighed Tess.

Next morning, when Tess and Nathan went to have breakfast, Mom and Dad were waiting for them at the table.

"Come and sit down," said Dad gently. "We've got something to tell you. Your mom and I have decided that it would be better if we didn't live together any more."

"You're going to get separated!" cried Tess. "Just like Jon's parents!" She felt the tears slide down her face.

Mom was in tears too. She put her arms around the children to comfort them. "It has been a difficult decision for Dad and me," she whispered. "You must feel so confused."

Nathan was angry! He pushed Mom's arm away, snatched his school lunch from the bench, and disappeared through the kitchen door. Tess picked up her backpack and raced after him.

"Wait!" called Dad, but they had already left.

At school, Nathan kept thinking about his Dad. Was he going to move out? Where would he live? And how would they manage without him?

Nathan's teacher came over to him. "Your mother called the school this morning, Nathan, to make sure you and Tess had arrived safely. Are you all right?" she asked gently.

Nathan shrugged his shoulders. "I'm okay," he said, but he sat in silence for the rest of the morning, feeling very unhappy.

Tess spent the day trying not to cry as she thought about Mom and Dad's decision. "It's not true! It's impossible!" she told herself, over and over again.

On the way home from school, Tess and Nathan stopped to talk. They sat on a wall, kicking their heels angrily against the bricks, while Nathan wiped his tears with the back of his hand.

Tess jumped down onto the sidewalk and said, "We'd better go home and see how Mom is. She looked really upset this morning."

"Dad looked sad, too," replied Nathan. "What can we do?"

"I don't know!" muttered Tess. "I wish things could be back the way they were."

The children walked slowly home. When they went inside, they found Dad busy in the kitchen.

"I came home early from work to see you," he told them. "I thought you'd probably be hungry after your hard day, so I'm making you both a sandwich."

Nathan ran to his dad and hugged him. "We love you!" he said.

"We love Mom, too," Tess added quickly.

"I know you do," said Dad.

Tess and Nathan and Dad sat down together at the table.

"What's going to happen, Dad?" Tess asked. "Are you going to move out?"

Dad nodded.

"Don't go too far away, please," said Nathan, fighting back more tears. "We want to come and see you."

Dad reached over and squeezed his arm. "Now, you mustn't worry! I can live with Grandma until I find a new house," he reassured them.

"Can we come and stay with you sometimes when you get your new house?" asked Tess.

"Of course you can," said Dad. "You will be staying lots of weekends. Sometimes we could go camping or fishing."

"Okay!" said Nathan. "That would be good."

"Yes!" said Tess, in a shaky voice, and she tried to smile, too.

At that moment, Mom came in through the front door. Tess and Nathan jumped up and gave her a hug. "Are you two all right?" she asked.

"We're feeling a bit better now, because Dad said he's going to be staying with Grandma for a while," said Tess.

"And we will be seeing him lots," said Nathan, blinking back his tears.

"I think we have two special children!" said Dad, looking at Mom.

Mom nodded her head and smiled. "Yes, we're very lucky," she said.

"And we'll still have our special mom and dad," said Tess. "Wherever you live, we'll always love you."

"And we'll always love you, too," said Mom and Dad.

"We know," said Nathan.